OCEAN HUNTERS

Written by Kris Hirschmann
Illustrated by Monika Popowitz

Copyright © 2000 by Troll Communications L.L.C.

Published by Troll Communications L.L.C.

Planet Reader is a trademark of Troll Communications L.L.C.

Printed in the United States of America.   ISBN 0-8167-6948-6

10   9   8   7   6   5   4   3   2

Welcome to Planet Reader!

Invite your child on a journey to a wonderful, imaginative place—
the limitless universe of reading! And there's no better traveling
companion than you, the parent. Every time you and your child read
together you send out an important message: Reading can be rewarding
and *fun*. This understanding is essential to helping your child build
the skills and confidence he or she needs as an emerging reader.

Here are some tips for sharing Planet Reader stories with your child:

Be open! Some children like to listen to or read the whole story and
then ask questions. Some children will stop on every page with a
question or a comment. Either way is fine; the most important thing
is that your child feels reading is a pleasurable experience.

Be understanding! Sometimes your child might need a direct answer.
If he or she points to a word and asks you to tell what it is, do so.
Other times, your child may want to sound out a word or stop to
figure out a sentence independently. Allow for both approaches.

Enjoy! This book was created especially for your child's age group.
Talk about the story. Take turns reading favorite parts. Look at how
the illustrations support the story and enhance the reading experience.

And most of all, enjoy your child's journey into literacy. It's one of the
most important trips the two of you will ever take!

Contents

Introduction
EAT OR BE EATEN

Every creature must eat to stay alive. Some animals eat only plants. But many hunt and eat other animals. These hunters are called *predators,* and the animals they eat are called *prey.*

In nature, almost every animal is food for another—even if that animal is a hunter! This is especially true in the ocean, which is full of animals of all shapes and sizes. A shrimp may be eaten by a small fish, which is eaten by a bigger fish, which is eaten by a dolphin, which is eaten by a shark. This is called the *food chain.* The biggest and most powerful predators, the ones with no natural enemies, are at the top of the food chain.

Prey is good at getting away, so many predators have developed special tricks. Some have amazing size or strength. Some have built-in weapons or cool disguises. And some are so strange that it's hard to believe they're real!

Get ready to take a fascinating journey into the underwater world of ocean hunters, where there's only one rule: Eat—or be eaten!

Killer Whale

Killer whales, or *orcas*, aren't true whales. They are a type of porpoise. They are very smart—and very good at outsmarting their prey.

Orcas may grow to 27 feet (8.2 m) and weigh 12,000 pounds (5,400 kg). With their size and speed, they can catch and eat almost any creature. Fish, dolphins, whales, seals, sea lions, walrus, squid, seabirds, and otters are all on the menu.

Orcas often hunt in *pods*, or groups. A pod can work together to kill large animals, such as whales. A pod can also swim in circles to trap a group of fish. One by one, each orca swims through the group, stunning dozens of fish with its powerful tail. Soon the pod has created a feast!

Orcas that hunt alone have tricks, too. An orca will poke its head out of the water to look for prey. If it spots a seal sitting on an ice floe, the orca may slide onto the ice, tipping it over. When the seal falls into the water, it's dinner time! An orca may even body surf onto a sand bar to grab a tasty bird or sea lion.

Many divers say orcas seem curious, not unfriendly, toward humans. They may even nibble gently on a diver's fins!

Humpback Whale

Humpback whales hunt in pods, too. Several of these 50-foot (15-m) giants swim around and around a school of fish, blowing bubbles and making loud noises. The frightened fish move close together. When the group of fish is tight enough, the whales lunge up through the center of the school with their mouths wide open. This trick, called *bubble netting*, lets a humpback catch thousands of fish in one gulp!

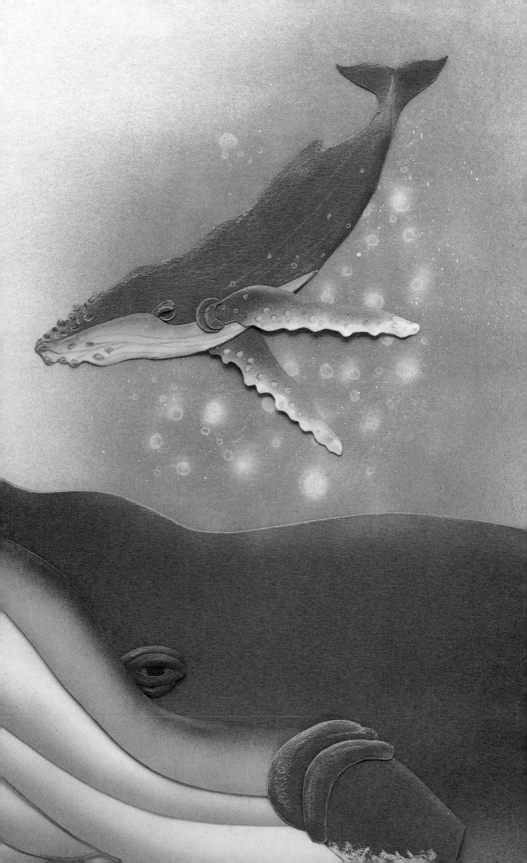

Giant Squid

A giant squid has never been captured alive. But we know they exist. They have been spotted many times, and their huge bodies have washed up on beaches around the world.

Scientists guess that a giant squid may measure up to 60 feet (18.3 m). The squid has eight long arms covered with 3-inch (7.5-cm) suckers. Each sucker is lined with sharp teeth so the squid can grab its prey (fish, clams, scallops, shrimp, or other squid). The squid also has two tentacles that it uses to stuff prey into its mouth. The mouth is a sharp beak so strong that it can cut through thick steel cable.

suckers

Giant squid live far below the ocean's surface, in places where little sunlight reaches. To see in the dark, the giant squid has the biggest eyes of any animal on Earth. Each eye is about 1 foot (30 cm) across!

Although you probably won't see a giant squid while swimming, they do come to the surface every now and then. This happens in the deep water far out in the ocean.

Sperm Whale

Sperm whales are the mortal enemies of giant squid. These 60-foot (18.3-m) hunters lurk in the deep waters where giant squid live, hoping for a meal. Many sperm whales are covered with scars—the results of their battles with giant squid. The whales usually win. We know this from their stomachs, which have been found to contain up to 10,000 squid beaks!

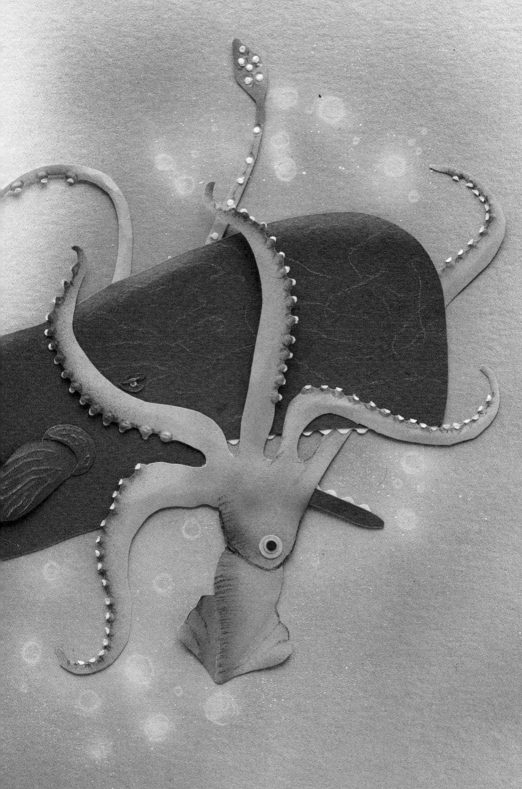

13

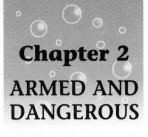

Chapter 2
ARMED AND DANGEROUS

Moray Eel

Moray eels are common on coral reefs around the world. They stick their heads out of holes in the coral, baring their sharp teeth. Although they look scary, they're not trying to be threatening. Morays must open and close their mouths to pump water through their bodies.

When it's time to hunt, though, those teeth come in handy. A moray prowls the reef like a snake, ducking into and out of nooks and crannies. When it finds its prey (mostly fish, crabs, lobsters, and octopuses), it strikes! The moray may also attack other predators that wander into its territory.

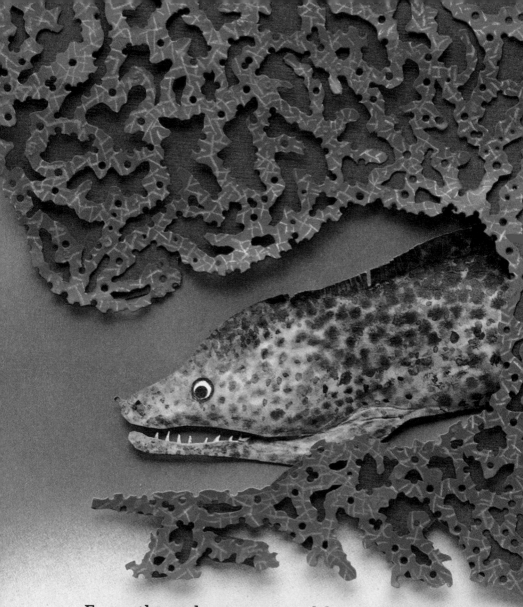

Even though morays seldom attack
people, they do sometimes bite if they feel
they are in danger. The bites are not fatal.
But the moray's flesh is poisonous if eaten,
so it can kill even after it has died!

Barracuda

At first glance, you wouldn't guess that barracuda are among the reef's most ferocious predators. These slender, silvery fish spend most of their time floating calmly, hardly moving. But their sharp eyes see everything. A flash of silver tells them that food (a small fish) is near. The barracuda goes from motionless to full speed in seconds, grabbing the prey with its strong jaws and jagged teeth.

An underwater barracuda encounter can be scary for a person. Barracuda are curious animals and often follow divers and snorkelers, watching their every move. As they watch, they slowly open and close their mouths. It looks like they're thinking about taking a bite! But humans are much too big to be prey for barracuda, which usually measure from 1 to 4 feet (30 cm to 1.2 m). Barracuda attack only if they see the glimmer of jewelry or other metal on a person's body. They sometimes mistake the silvery shine for a fish.

Marlin

The marlin is a skilled predator in its ocean home. This huge animal measures up to 14 feet (4.25 m) and may weigh up to 2,000 pounds (900 kg). Its size, strength, and speed have earned it the nickname "lion of the sea."

Able to swim at speeds over 50 miles per hour (80 kph), the marlin is one of the fastest fish in the ocean. It needs the speed to catch its favorite food, tuna, which can swim up to 45 miles per hour (72 kph). Marlin sometimes also hunt in pods, herding fish into a ball. Scientists think they may communicate by flashing lights along their sides, signaling what they plan to do.

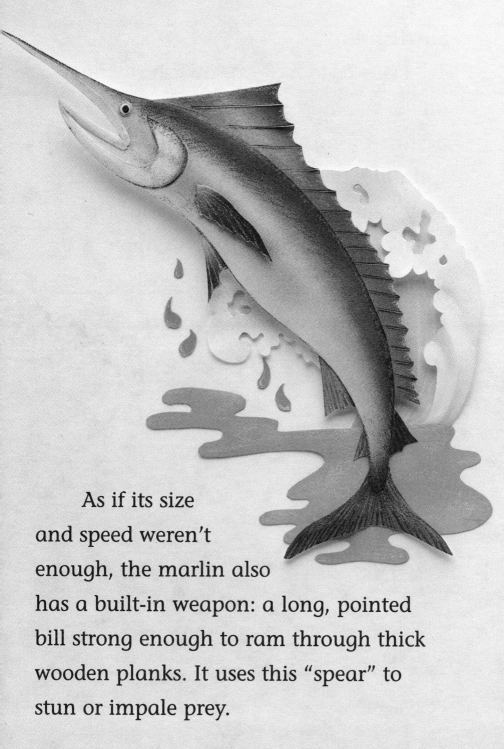

As if its size
and speed weren't
enough, the marlin also
has a built-in weapon: a long, pointed
bill strong enough to ram through thick
wooden planks. It uses this "spear" to
stun or impale prey.

Sawfish Ray

The 20-foot (6-m) sawfish ray has one of the most unusual noses in the ocean: a long "saw" called a *rostra*. Sharp teeth line the edges of the rostra, which may be up to 6 feet (1.8 m) long. The sawfish uses this fearsome weapon to stir up the sandy bottom, then slash any prey it uncovers.

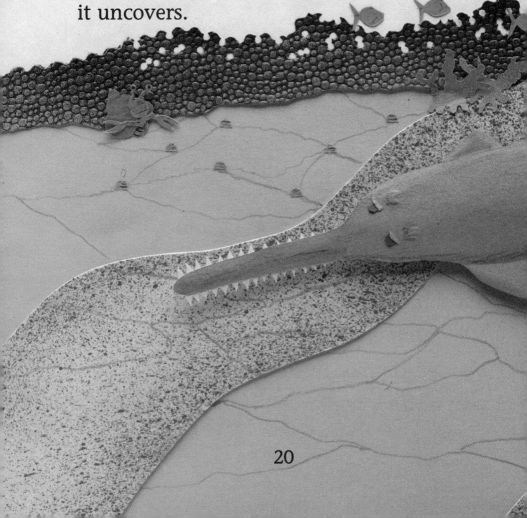

Sadly, some people think the sawfish's amazing nose should be a trophy. As a result, the sawfish has been hunted nearly to the point of extinction.

Chapter 3
SHARKS: NATURE'S PERFECT PREDATORS

Sharks have terrorized the seas for more than 300 million years. Ocean creatures have much to fear from these powerful hunters, who are sometimes called "nature's perfect predators."

Before a shark can kill prey, it must find it. Using their keen sense of smell, sharks can detect the tiniest drop of blood in water. Then they "sniff" along the trail to a wounded animal. As the shark gets closer, it listens for movement in the water. The shark's skin also contains special organs called *lateral lines* that can sense disturbances in the water.

When the shark gets really close, it uses sensors around its nose to pick up the weak electrical fields of its prey. Using these sensors, sharks can find even buried or hidden animals.

Finally, the shark spots its prey and attacks! Its warm blood gives it extra energy for speed. And because it has rubbery cartilage instead of bones, the shark can turn with amazing speed while it chases its dinner.

As it moves in for the kill, the shark depends on its most powerful weapon: its teeth. A shark has several rows of razor-sharp teeth that can easily shred prey. If one tooth falls out during an attack, another one quickly pops into place. A shark may lose and replace thousands of teeth in a lifetime.

Let's take a look at a few of these fearsome predators.

Great White Shark

Great white sharks are feared around the world.

Their size alone is scary. Great whites usually measure 14 to 18 feet (4.3 to 5.5 m), but they may grow to 21 feet (6.4 m) and 4,000 pounds (1,800 kg). That's a lot of shark!

Along with the big body, great whites have huge mouths full of 3-inch (7.5-cm) teeth. The sharks use these knifelike teeth to slice through the skin and bones of their prey—squid, whales, turtles, seals, and other sharks. Great whites have even eaten horses and elephants that strayed into shallow water.

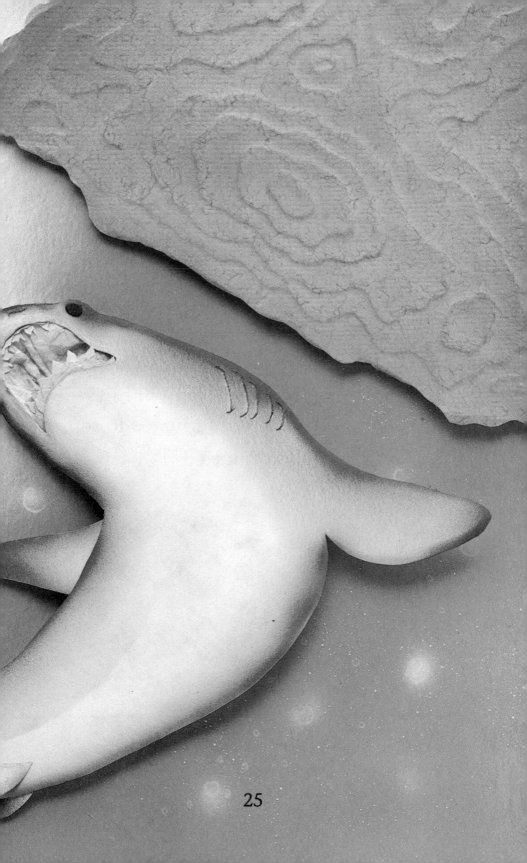

Hammerhead Shark

Hammerheads are easy to recognize. Their flat heads look just like hammers. Scientists aren't sure why hammerheads have such unusually shaped heads. But they have several ideas. Some think the head provides "lift," making it easier for the sharks to swim. Others think having widely spaced eyes improves the sharks' vision. Still others think the broad head makes it easier for hammerheads to sense the electrical fields of buried prey.

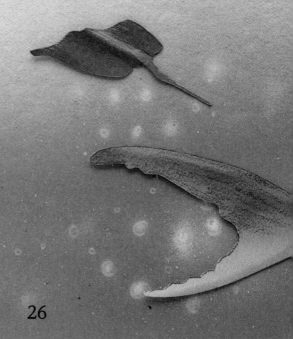

One thing is for sure. Hammerheads have no trouble finding their favorite food: stingrays. They dig up the stingrays from the ocean floor, then batter them with their heads. A hammerhead was once found with 95 stingray barbs attached to its chin!

Hammerheads sometimes travel in large schools. Would you want to be surrounded by dozens of these hungry sharks?

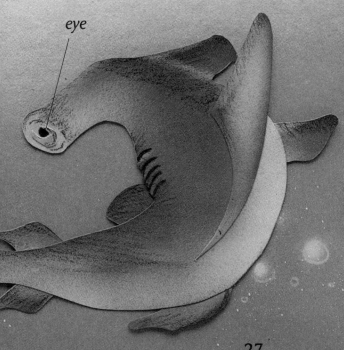

eye

Bull Shark

The bull shark isn't all that large—it measures about 10 feet (3 m) long. But it is the most dangerous shark to man. People swimming in shallow waters are sometimes bitten by bull sharks, which are very aggressive. Bull sharks can even live in fresh water and are sometimes found in rivers, far from the ocean. Bull sharks will eat almost anything, including other sharks. Their diet also includes fish, turtles, dolphins, and birds.

Chapter 4

DEADLY DISGUISES

Trumpetfish

Trumpetfish live on coral reefs around the world. These slender predators measure about 20 inches (51 cm). Trumpetfish stand on their heads among coral branches to hide themselves. They can even change color to better match their surroundings.

Small fish, crabs, or octopuses are often fooled by this disguise. When one of these animals strays too close, the trumpetfish opens its large mouth, sucks the prey in, and swallows it whole!

Octopus

Octopuses measure anywhere from 1 inch (2.5 cm) to 28 feet (8.5 m). They can change color by making special cells in their skin bigger or smaller. Changing color helps the octopus blend into the background as it waits for dinner to swim by.

An octopus prowls the coral reef, poking its eight arms into holes. It uses its suckers (up to 240 on each arm) to taste any animal it finds. If the animal tastes good, the octopus grabs it by creating a vacuum seal with its suckers. The unlucky prey is then pulled out of the hole.

Once the prey is caught, the octopus has several deadly tricks. It may close its body around the prey, then release poison to stun the animal. It may peck the prey to death with its sharp beak. Or it may use its strong arms to strangle the animal. If the prey is a shellfish, the octopus drills a hole through the shell with its tooth-covered tongue. It shoots powerful juices into the hole. The juices dissolve the creature, then the octopus slurps up the remains through the hole.

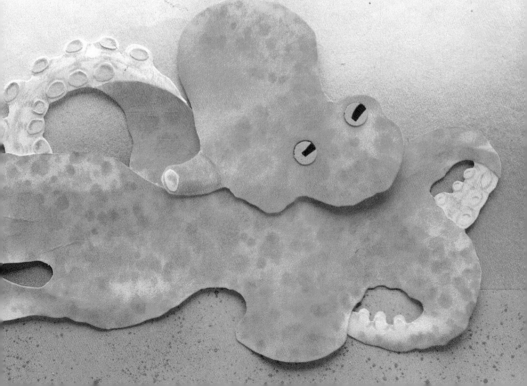

Frogfish

Frogfish may be the best-disguised of all ocean hunters. Their lumpy bodies look like bumps on a coral reef, and they can change color to match their environment. Frogfish blend in so well, they sometimes hunt the same area for months without being noticed by other animals.

Frogfish are small—no longer than 5 inches (13 cm)—but they are deadly. They can suck prey into their mouths in a fraction of a second, and they are able to swallow animals larger than themselves.

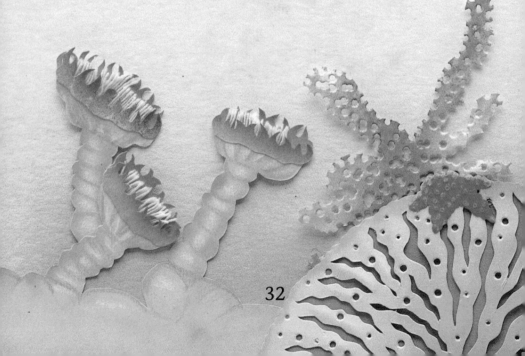

Frogfish are a type of *anglerfish*, which means they fish for their food. They attract prey by dangling built-in lures called *esca* in front of their mouths. An esca often looks like a worm or a tiny fish. When larger fish try to make a meal of the esca, they quickly discover that *they* are the ones about to be eaten.

Chapter 5
DRIFTING DANGER

Jellyfish

Jellyfish aren't the most active creatures in the ocean. They simply hang in the water, drifting wherever the currents take them. So how do they catch prey? They let it come to them!

Many jellyfish have *tentacles*—long, stringlike "fingers" that dangle in the water. Each tentacle is lined with stinging cells. When a fish or a shrimp bumps into these cells, tiny stingers are released. The jagged barbs easily pierce the prey's flesh. Poison is then pumped into the animal through thin, flexible tubes that connect the barbs to the jellyfish's body. The tentacles pull the paralyzed prey up to the jellyfish's mouth, where it is eaten.

It's easy to see why these predators are so deadly despite their slowpoke ways. Many jellies have transparent bodies, so other animals seldom see them until it's too late.

The world's biggest jellyfish drifts in the cold waters of the Arctic Ocean. It is called the *lion's mane,* and its head may be up to 7 feet (2 m) across. A fringe of up to 1,200 poisonous tentacles surrounds the large head. Each tentacle may be as long as 120 feet (36.6 m)!

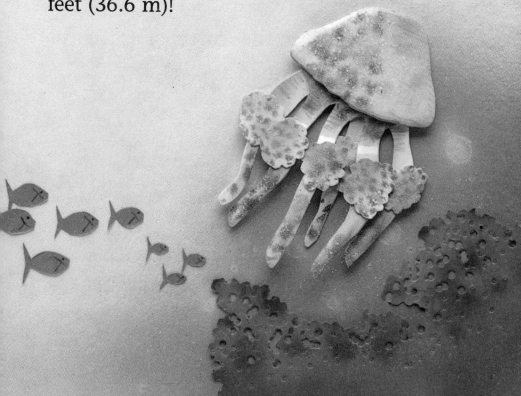

The *beroe cucumis* (bear-ROW-ee kyu-KYU-miss) is a jellyfish that looks like a cucumber but acts like a swimming stomach. It prowls the deep ocean waters, hoping to bump into food (usually another jelly). When it does, it opens its gigantic mouth and swallows the animal whole!

The *sea wasp* jellyfish is the most poisonous animal in the world. A sting from one of its 60 tentacles can kill a person in 30 seconds. Just imagine what it can do to smaller creatures! This deadly hunter is found in the waters of northern Australia and southeast Asia.

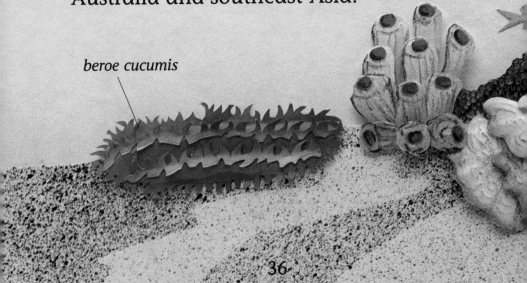

beroe cucumis

sea wasp —————

37

Portuguese Man-of-War

The Portuguese man-of-war's "head" is a colorful, gas-filled bubble that floats on top of the water. This makes it easy to spot from up above. But from underwater, this creature is nearly invisible. Because its body floats, fish and shrimp don't see the man-of-war until they are tangled in its long tentacles. These deadly fingers, which contain enough poison to kill a person, trail up to 165 feet (50 m) behind the man-of-war's body.

Because it is so hard to see, the man-of-war is a great hunter. And it doesn't even have to try. Its bubble acts like a sail; the man-of-war travels wherever the wind takes it, waiting to bump into food.

Many people think
the Portuguese man-of-war
is a jellyfish. But it's not.
It is a colony of small
creatures called *polyps*
(POL-ips). Each polyp
has a job to do. Some sting, some eat,
some maintain the bubble, and some are
in charge of making new men-of-war.

Gulper Eel

As the ocean gets deeper, sunlight fades away and animal life becomes scarcer and scarcer. But despite the lack of food, many predators lurk in these dark depths. One odd-looking deep-sea hunter is the 5-foot (1.5-m) gulper eel. This creature is named for its gigantic mouth. When open, this mouth is much wider than the eel's body. The eel can even unhinge its jaws to eat extra-large animals.

40

The eel's body looks small in comparison with its mouth. But this creature has no trouble digesting its prey. The body is elastic and can stretch to hold fish much larger than itself. Why does the gulper eel eat such big creatures? In the deep ocean, food is so scarce that a predator may die if a meal gets away. So nature has made sure the gulper eel can eat almost any prey, no matter how big.

Mantis Shrimp

Most shrimp are harmless. But not the mantis shrimp. At 10 inches (25 cm), the mantis is bigger than most shrimp—and far nastier.

The mantis shrimp has two arms, each ending in a powerful claw. The shrimp holds these arms folded beneath its head. It looks a lot like a praying mantis, which is how it gets its name.

The mantis buries itself in sand, waiting for worms, shrimp, fish, snails, or crabs to wander by. When prey appears, the mantis thrusts its claws out with lightning speed. The mantis can kill its victim in just three-thousandths of a second! The prey is either speared or clubbed to death.

Mantis shrimp are strong, too. Their strike can split a person's flesh to the bone. In some parts of the world, these dangerous hunters are called "thumb splitters" because of the damage they can do.

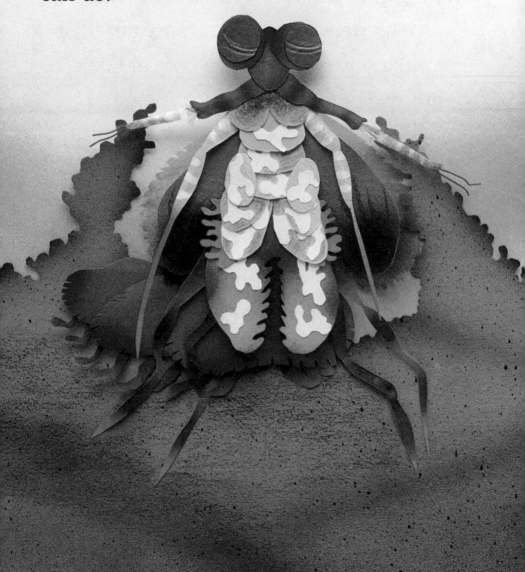

Sea Star

Sea stars are sometimes called *starfish*. There are hundreds of varieties, and they are found all over the world. Sea stars may be as small as ½ inch (1.2 cm) or as large as 3 feet (91 cm).

Sea stars take their name from their starlike shape. They have central bodies with five or more arms that spread outward. Each arm has hundreds of tiny tube feet that help the sea star to walk.

Most sea stars are slow; they may travel just 1 inch (2.5 cm) in an hour. But that doesn't stop them from hunting for their favorite foods. When a sea star finds a clam or an oyster, it wraps its arms around the prey and holds tight. It pulls and pulls until the prey weakens and its shell opens a crack. The sea star then pushes its stomach out of its mouth and

into the shell, where it digests the prey.
When the sea star is finished, it pulls
its stomach back into its body and
walks away, leaving an empty
shell behind.

Instead of shellfish, the *crown-of-thorns* sea star eats coral polyps. It travels slowly over the reef, munching as it goes. The crown-of-thorns can be large—up to 3 feet (90 cm) across—and its 16 arms are covered with poisonous spikes.

A football-sized ocean snail called a *triton* is one of the few animals that will attack the crown-of-thorns. The triton sucks one of the sea star's arms into its shell. It injects paralyzing poison, then flips the crown-of-thorns over and feasts on its belly.

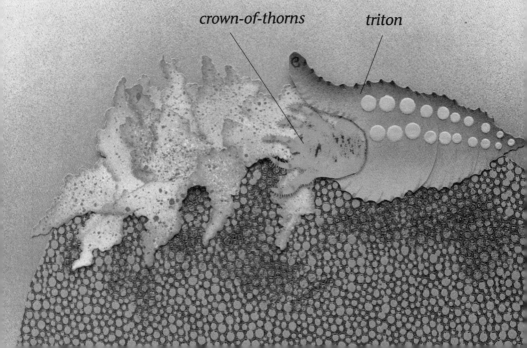

crown-of-thorns   triton

Conclusion

Predators are the most powerful creatures in the ocean. But being at the top of the food chain puts these animals in great danger. If the ocean's balance changes and smaller creatures begin to die, the larger predators may starve.

People, the deadliest hunters of all, are changing the ocean's balance by overfishing and polluting. Can we stop before the changes are permanent? Or will we keep going, slowly destroying species that took millions of years to evolve? Only time will tell.

Index